MAKE & DO
CHRISTMAS
PUPPET
PLAYS

Includes 10 easy-to-perform puppet plays

Standard PUBLISHING
Bringing The Word to Life
Cincinnati, Ohio

Jane Martin-Scott
and Gillian Chapman

CONTENTS

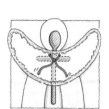

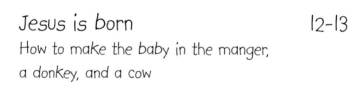

HOW TO USE THIS BOOK

Make and Do Christmas Puppet Plays is designed for groups to work on together to produce the props and perform the plays that make up the story of Jesus' birth.

This book offers play scripts to enable a cast of characters to reenact the events of the first Christmas, and it also provides detailed instructions for making the puppets for the presentation.

The play

The play scripts are designed to take children right through the Christmas story, from the annunciation to the wise men's worship of Jesus. There are instructions for all the puppets to be made to accompany the play script. All can be adapted to the number of children available to make them or the time available for the play performance.

The puppets

The puppets are quite large and they have interchangeable costumes and features. Although a class of children might want to make each one different and unique, a family might equally make the presentation work well by adapting or swapping clothing and props between play scenes.

The costumes for the puppets can be made using scraps of leftover material or old curtains, bedding, or table linen available at home or by using recycled clothing or other fabrics from charity shops. Everything from old shirts, jumpers, and denim jeans to accessories, buttons, and costume jewelry could be used to make the puppets fun and interesting to look at.

The performance

Make this Christmas a traditional one, with the birth of Jesus at its center. Whether at home, in school, or in church, there are many opportunities to celebrate Christmas with a tableau of Christ's birth in a stable in Bethlehem.

HOW TO MAKE ONE BASIC PUPPET

These are the instructions for making all the puppet people. Once made, there are special instructions to dress and decorate them so they become men, women, and angels. The wooden spoon provides a handle to hold and manipulate the puppet.

How to make the puppet body

1 Cover the oval card stock with a smooth layer of glue. Place the card stock, glue-side down, on top of the felt and firmly rub down on the card stock with your hand, making sure the edges are stuck firmly.

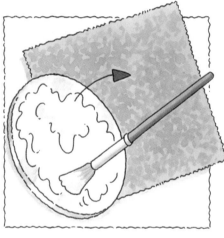

3 Glue the wooden spoon or spatula to the back of the card stock. Leave to dry until stuck firmly.

2 When the card stock is completely dry, cut away the extra felt.

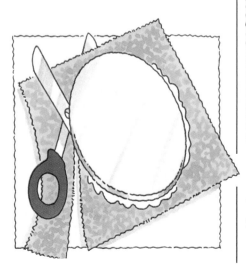

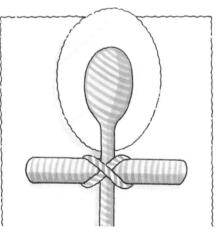

4 Attach the short length of dowel across the spoon handle to form the puppet's shoulders. Wind string across the joint to hold the dowel securely, then brush the string with glue to strengthen the joint. Leave to dry.

You will need:

Strong, thick card stock, cut into an oval shape, approx 6" x 8"

Light brown felt

Wooden spoon or spatula

Wooden dowel, approx 9" x ½" thick

String and scissors

Glue and brush

Fabric for dress or robe, 16" square

hook-and-loop fasteners

Needle and thread

How to make a robe or dress and coat

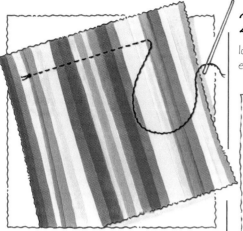

1 Cut a piece of plain or striped fabric 16" square. Knot the end of the length of thread and sew a row of simple running stitches along the fabric 1" from the top.

2 Pull the thread to gather the fabric and tie the ends firmly. Attach the hook-and-loop fasteners to either side of the fabric at each end of the row of stitches.

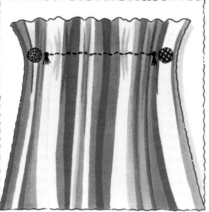

3 Wrap the fabric around the basic puppet body and join together using the hook-and-loop fasteners. Leave the opening at the back so you can use the handle and manipulate the puppet.

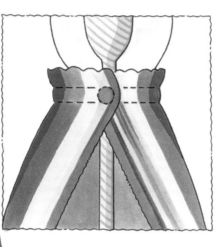

4 To make a coat, fold a piece of fabric around the puppet before the arms are attached. Glue or sew the fabric to the top of the main dress.

How to make the sleeves

Fold two pieces of fabric, each half the length of the dowel, to make two arms. Cut out two felt hands and glue them inside the arms. Glue or sew the arms to the costume.

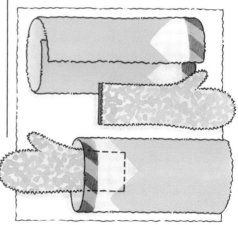

THE ANGEL VISITS MARY

Over 2,000 years ago, in a town called Nazareth, there lived a girl named Mary. Mary was engaged to Joseph, the carpenter, who was descended from King David, the great king of Israel.

One day, Mary had an unexpected visitor.

"Mary!" he said. "My name is Gabriel. I am an angel come from God with a message for you."

Mary was terrified. Why would God be interested in a poor girl like her?

"Do not be afraid, Mary," the angel spoke again. "God is very pleased with you. He's going to send his Son into the world. And he has chosen you to be his mother. You will call him Jesus."

"But how can I become a mother?" Mary asked. "I am not even married yet."

"God will send his Holy Spirit and you will be blessed with God's own Son," said Gabriel. "Nothing is impossible for God. Remember your cousin Elizabeth? She is soon to have a baby—and she is well past the age for having children."

Mary was amazed. But she knew she could trust God.

"I am a servant of the Lord," she said. "Let everything happen just as you have said."

Then, just as suddenly as he had appeared, Gabriel left her.

How to make the angel

1 Make the basic puppet using the instructions on page 4.

2 Cut a semicircle of card stock 1 ½" wider than the puppet's head. Cover with white silk fabric, securing with glue or taping the fabric at the back.

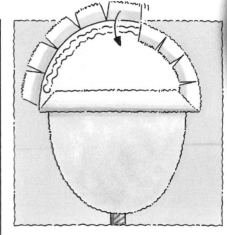

You will need:

✂

White silk fabric for headdress

Pale yellow cotton fabric, 16" sq.

Small pieces of yellow fabric for arms

Scissors, needle, and thread

Pieces of felt or card stock for features

hook-and-loop fasteners (small tabs or strips cut to size)

Large pieces of white card stock (for wings and headdress)

Several pieces of sparkly net fabric

Glue, string, and masking tape

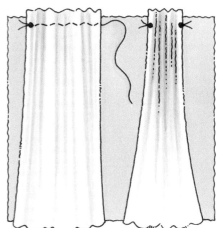

3 Cut two pieces of the white silk fabric 4" x 10". Gather them at the top with running stitches, then pull until 1" wide and secure.

4 Glue them to each side of the card stock and leave to dry.

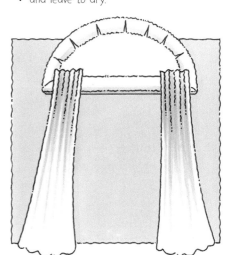

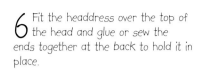

6 Fit the headdress over the top of the head and glue or sew the ends together at the back to hold it in place.

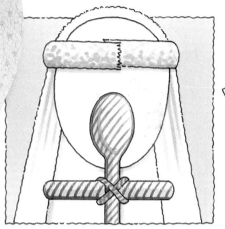

7 Knot the end of a length of thread and sew running stitches along the yellow fabric 1" from the top. Pull the thread to gather the fabric and tie the ends. Attach the hook-and-loop fasteners to the fabric at each end of the stitches.

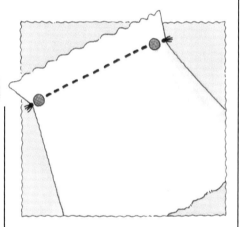

8 Sew the sparkly net fabric to the top of the yellow dress with simple stitches.

9 Fold two pieces of yellow fabric to make the arms (see pages 4 and 5 for further instructions). Cut out two felt hands and glue them inside the arms. Glue or sew the arms to the back of the costume.

10 Cut the facial features from pieces of felt or card stock and attach hook-and-loop fasteners to the back of each. Position the corresponding part of the hook-and-loop fasteners to the face so the features can be placed accurately.

11 To make the wings, sketch the wing shape on a large piece of white card stock, making sure they are symmetrical and large enough to be seen on either side of the angel's body.

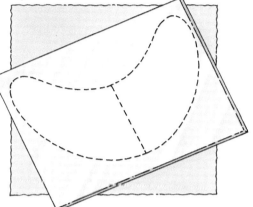

12 Cut out the wings and cover them with sparkly net. Lay the net down on a flat surface, then place the card wings on top. Fold the net on to the back of the card stock and hold in place with masking tape and glue. Leave to dry, then remove the tape.

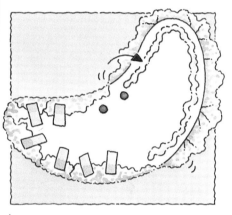

13 Make two holes in the card stock wings as shown. Tie a length of string to the wooden spoon handle, thread the string through the holes, and knot to hold the wings in place.

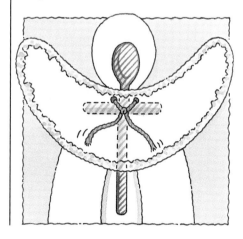

5 Glue a 16" band of white silk fabric across the front of the head-dress, covering the tops of the two side pieces of fabric.

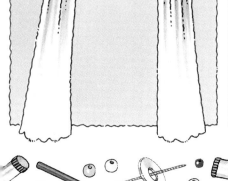

THE ROAD TO BETHLEHEM

When Joseph heard Mary's story about the angel and found that she was going to have a baby, he was not sure what to think. But God sent an angel to speak to Joseph in a dream and assure him that this was part of God's plan.

Now it was near the time for the baby to be born. But instead of settling down to wait for his birth, Mary and Joseph had to make a long journey.

The emperor, who was called Caesar Augustus, had ordered a census of all his people. Everyone in his kingdom had to be counted and put on a register. Then the Roman rulers would know where everybody was, so that they could call on them to serve in the army and pay their taxes. As Joseph was Jewish, he wouldn't have to serve in the army—but he would still have to pay his taxes!

Mary and Joseph had to travel back to his family's home town of Bethlehem, some miles from Nazareth. They started their journey; a dusty, tiring trip for Mary, who became more and more uncomfortable.

When they arrived in Bethlehem, Mary knew her baby would soon be born.

You will need:

Stiff card stock

Scissors

Different kinds of blue fabric

Sticky tape or glue

Blue buttons

How to make Mary

1 Follow the basic puppet instructions on pages 4 and 5. Give Mary blue buttons for eyes. To make the coat, fold a piece of blue fabric around the puppet before the arms are attached. Glue or sew the fabric to the top of the main dress.

2 Cut a narrow semicircle of card stock in the shape of a headband, following the shape of Mary's head. Cover with blue fabric, gluing in place or taping the fabric at the back.

3 Cut the headdress from the blue fabric and fold in half to find the middle. Glue the edges of the head band to the middle of the fabric. Leave to dry before fitting over Mary's head.

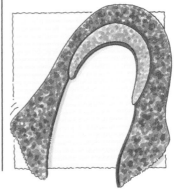

How to make Joseph

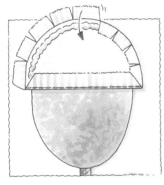

1 Follow the basic puppet instructions on pages 4 and 5. Give Joseph brown buttons for eyes. Cut a semicircle of card stock 1 ½" wider than his head. Cover with fabric, securing with glue or taping the fabric at the back.

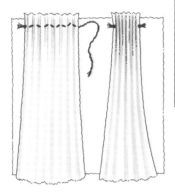

2 Cut two pieces of fabric 4" x 10". Gather them at the top with running stitches, then pull until 1" wide and secure.

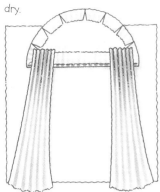

3 Glue them to each side of the card stock and leave to dry.

4 Glue a 16" band of fabric across the front of the headdress, covering the tops of the two side pieces of fabric.

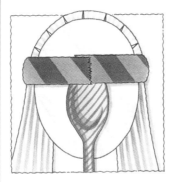

5 Fit the headdress over the top of the head and glue or sew the ends together at the back to hold it in place.

You will need:

✂

Stiff card stock

Scissors

Striped fabric

Sticky tape or glue

Needle and thread

Brown buttons

Burlap

String

Strong embroidery thread or shoe lace

How to make Joseph's bag

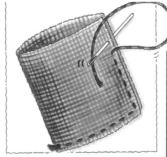

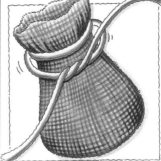

1 Cut out a rectangle of burlap and fold in half. Sew together the bottom and open side edges with running stitches, leaving open the top end.

2 Tie a length of string, embroidery thread, or shoe lace around the open end of the bag to gather it closed. Tuck it behind Joseph's arm and glue in place.

FULLY BOOKED!

Bethlehem was busy—much busier than they had expected. There didn't seem to be anywhere for Mary and Joseph to stay. Every inn and hostel was full to bursting.

Mary was feeling more and more uncomfortable. Joseph went up to the door of another inn and knocked loudly.

"Sorry, no room!" said the innkeeper, as he opened the door. "We're all full up."

"Wait!" Joseph said as the innkeeper turned to go. "Please—we just need somewhere under cover. My wife is about to have a baby."

The innkeeper turned back and looked at them both. He could see that Mary couldn't go on much further.

"I'm sorry—all my rooms are taken—but I can offer you the stable at the back. It's where I keep the animals, so it doesn't smell too good but it's dry. You can stay there if you want."

Joseph quickly accepted the innkeeper's offer. They hurried around the back. It was as they had been told—there were oxen, sheep, and chickens, but Mary and Joseph were just pleased to have somewhere to stay for the night.

How to make the innkeeper

1 Make the basic puppet using the instructions on pages 4 and 5. Cut a piece of plain or striped fabric 16" square. Knot the end of a length of thread and sew a row of simple running stitches along the fabric 1" from the top.

2 Decorate the innkeeper's robe with an apron made from pieces of burlap, attaching it at the back with safety pins. Attach straps with small buttons sewn in place as shown.

3 Cut out nose, ears, and mouth from felt or thin card. Attach these to a felt beard if you want to swap from one character to another.

How to make the innkeeper's hat

1 Fold a strip of fabric that fits across the top of the innkeeper's head. Glue the fabric together at the back.

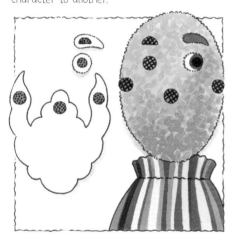

4 Attach hook-and-loop fasteners to the back of two matching buttons to make the eyes, and add eyebrows cut from felt or card stock. Position the corresponding part of the fastener carefully on the face so the features can be placed accurately.

2 Wind wool around a thin piece of card stock to make a simple tassel. Pass a small length of yarn under the wound wool and knot tightly before removing the card stock. Wrap wool around the top of the tassel and cut through the loops. Attach the tassel to the hat as shown.

You will need:

✂

Plain and striped fabrics, burlap, and string

Colorful, silky, and patterned fabrics and trimmings

Scissors, needle, and strong thread

Glue and brush

Buttons and brown or black wool

Pieces of felt and card stock

Hook-and-loop fasteners (small tabs or strips cut to size)

Safety pins

JESUS IS BORN

Mary and Joseph had travelled a long way. They were dirty and tired. But there was little rest for them that night.

Some time during the night, Mary gave birth to her first baby, a son, God's own child. There was no one else there to greet him—just Joseph and a handful of animals.

"What do we do now, Mary?" Joseph asked.

"I'll wrap him in these cloths," Mary replied.

"Look, you can put him here in the manger. There's clean straw. The animals can eat out of something else. Maybe he can sleep there."

So Mary put her baby in the manger.

"What shall we call him?" asked Joseph.

"Jesus," answered Mary. "His name is Jesus. The angel who came to see me told me his name."

So there they were, safe and dry—Mary, Joseph, and the baby Jesus in the manger.

You will need:

Stiff card stock

Scissors

Paints and brush, or brown paper

Glue and brush

Raffia or straw

Wooden spoon

Brown felt for face

Scraps of felt for hair and features

Two buttons for the eyes

Strips of yellow fabric

How to make the baby in the manger

1 Cut out a manger shape from the stiff card stock. Either paint the card stock to look like wood or cover it with brown paper. Glue the wooden spoon to the back of the manger to use as a handle.

2 Glue pieces of raffia or straw to the top of the manger, and leave to dry.

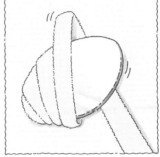

3 Cut out an oval of card stock to make Jesus' body. Cover with glue. Wrap with strips of yellow fabric.

4 Cut out a piece of round card stock for the face and cover with a smooth layer of glue. Place the card stock glue-side down on top of the felt and rub down firmly on the card stock with your hand, especially around the edges. Leave to dry, then cut off the excess felt.

5 Cut out the hair and features from felt and glue them to the face. Glue on button eyes. When dry, glue the body in place over the straw and glue the head to the body.

You will need:

✂️

Strong card stock

Scissors

Glue and brush

Grey and brown felt

Pieces of cord, felt, wool, leather, cloth, and buttons

A wooden spoon

How to make a donkey

1 Cut out a simple shape of a donkey's head from strong card stock and cover with a smooth layer of glue. Place the head, glue-side down, on top of grey felt and firmly rub down on the piece with your hand, making sure the edges are stuck firmly.

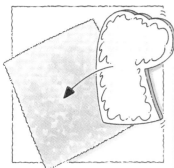

2 Cut long ears from card stock and cover with felt. Cut eyes, eyebrows, muzzle, and mane from scraps of felt and wool.

3 Glue the wooden spoon to the back of the donkey's head. Use thick cord to make a bridle as shown.

How to make a cow

1 Cut out the shape of the cow's head from strong card stock. Cover with a smooth layer of glue. Place the head, glue-side down, on top of brown felt and firmly rub down on the piece, especially around the edges.

2 When the glue is dry, trim off the excess felt.

3 Cut out the ears, horns, muzzle, and other features from card stock, felt, or leather cloth, and glue in place. Glue on buttons for eyes.

4 Glue the wooden spoon to the back of the cow to act as a handle.

SHEPHERDS ON THE HILLSIDE

Although Bethlehem was full of people, the countryside around the town was quiet, with just a few shepherds tending to their flocks of sheep. They took turns to watch the animals, so that no sheep would stray or be taken by wolves.

Suddenly the sky lit up as if it were on fire! The shepherds fell to the ground and half covered their eyes as high above them an angel appeared.

"Do not be afraid," the angel said. "I have wonderful news for you and the whole world. Today in Bethlehem, a baby has been born who is Christ the Lord. Go there and you will find him wrapped in swaddling clothes and lying in a manger."

Before the shepherds could catch their breath, the sky was filled with more and more angels.

"Glory to God in the highest," they sang. "Peace and joy to everyone on earth." Then, almost as quickly as they appeared, they were gone. The shepherds slowly looked around them. "That was amazing!" one said. "Yes," answered another, "but just think how amazing it is if what they said is true!"

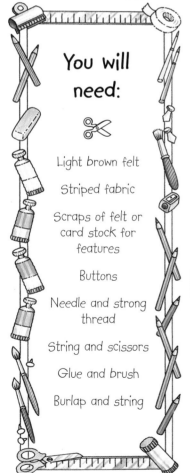

You will need:

✂

Light brown felt

Striped fabric

Scraps of felt or card stock for features

Buttons

Needle and strong thread

String and scissors

Glue and brush

Burlap and string

How to make a shepherd

1 Make the basic puppet using the instructions on pages 4 and 5.

2 Cut out nose, ears, and mouth from felt or thin card stock. Attach these to a felt beard if you want to swap from one character to another.

How to make a bag and cloak

1 Fold a piece of burlap into three parts to make a bag. Sew the edges together, leaving the top part open. Fold the top down to close the bag and sew on a button and loop of thread to secure it. Loop a piece of string through the bag long enough to wear over the shepherd's shoulder.

2 Use different fabrics for each of the shepherds. Drape pieces of burlap or old knit fabric around the body to make a cloak and tie at the shoulder or secure with a large button.

How to make a shepherd's headdress

1 Cut a semicircle of card stock 1½" wider than the head. Cover with striped fabric, either gluing in place, or taping the fabric at the back. When the card stock is dry, cut away the extra felt.

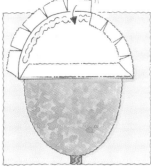

2 Cut two pieces of fabric 4" x 10". Gather them at the top with running stitches, then pull until 1" wide and secure.

3 Glue them to each side of the card stock and leave to dry.

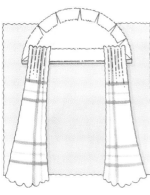

4 Glue a 16" band of fabric across the front of the headdress, covering the tops of the two side pieces of fabric.

5 Fit the headdress over the top of the head and glue or sew the ends together at the back to hold it in place.

How to make a sheep

1 Cut out a simple shape of a sheep's head from thick grey or white card stock and cover with a smooth layer of glue. Place the card stock, glue-side down, on top of the felt and firmly rub down on the card stock with your hand, making sure the edges are stuck firmly.

2 Cut short ears from card stock and cover with black felt. Cut eyes from scraps of felt.

3 Cut four sheep legs from card stock, cover with white felt, and attach to the body with paper fasteners. Pierce the card stock first with a sharp pencil before pushing the paper fastener through. Cut feet, nose, tail from card stock, cover with felt, and add as shown.

4 Glue the wooden spoon to the back of the sheep's body.

You will need:

Strong card stock

A wooden spoon

Pieces of card stock

Black and white felt

Buttons

Glue and brush

Scissors

Sharp pencil

Paper fasteners for moving legs

THE LONG JOURNEY

A long way from Bethlehem, some very clever men were puzzling about the appearance of a new star in the sky. It was brighter than the others and they couldn't remember seeing it before. They decided that the new star must be a sign—a sign that a new king had been born.

First, they packed gifts fit for a king: gold, a sign of riches and royalty; frankincense, the sign of a priest; and myrrh, for burial, a sign of what would briefly happen to Jesus.

Then they packed their bags and started on their long journey—a journey to find the new baby king, guided by the star.

2 Make a hat by folding a strip of silky fabric and securing it with glue at the back.

3 Gather and tuck a piece of creased, scrunched silky fabric into the top and sew or glue it in place.

How to make the wise men

You will need:

✄

Scissors

Glue and brush

Silky, patterned fabrics

Gold braids, lace, and ribbons

Costume jewelry and sequins

Felt scraps

Matching buttons

Pieces of felt or card stock for features

Safety pins

1 Make the basic puppets by following the instructions on pages 4 and 5. Vary the color and shapes of their features so that the eyes, eyebrows, and beards of the wise men are different from the innkeeper and shepherds. For the coats, use silky, patterned fabrics, trimmed with gold braids for their clothes. Decorate them with pieces of costume jewelry.

How to make a star

You will need:

✂

A sheet of gold holographic card stock

Pair of compasses

Scissors

Pencil and ruler

Glue and brush

Curly gold ribbon and yellow tissue paper

Wooden spoon

Strong thread

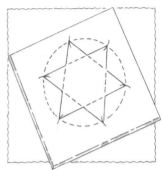

1 Draw a large circle on the back of the holographic card stock with the compasses. Divide the circle up and draw two overlapping triangles. Cut out the star carefully.

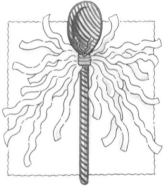

2 Cut lengths of curly ribbon and scrunch up thin strips of yellow tissue paper. Tie them together as shown and tie them to the top of the wooden spoon with the thread.

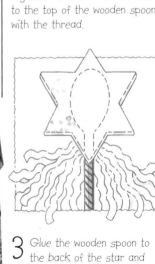

3 Glue the wooden spoon to the back of the star and leave to dry.

4 Make a turban by cutting a length of fabric that matches a wise man's costume and twist it around his head.

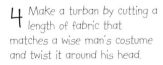

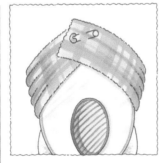

5 Hold the turban in place at the back with a safety pin.

THE WISE MEN MEET KING HEROD

King Herod was a cruel and ruthless ruler. He was surprised by the visit of the wise men, looking for a baby king. He wanted no one else to be his rival for the position of king. He called for his chief priests.

"Where do your writings tell you that this new king is to be born?" he asked.

"The prophets say that the Messiah is to be born in Bethlehem, in Judea," they replied.

King Herod told the wise men to go and look for the baby in Bethlehem. But just as they were about to leave, he asked them to return and tell him when they found the baby—so that he could worship him also.

The wise men continued their journey, leaving Herod to think about what he would do when he learned where this new threat to him was to be found.

You will need:

Holographic card stock

Scissors

Glue and brush

Silky, patterned fabrics

Gold braids, lace, and ribbons

Costume jewelry and sequins

Felt scraps

Matching buttons

Velvet and other fabric

Needle and thread

Embroidery thread or shoe lace

Darning needle

How to make King Herod

1 Follow the basic puppet instructions on pages 4 and 5. For the coat, use silky patterned fabrics and decorate them with gold braid, buttons, and trimmings.

2 Make angry facial features and glue them in place. Follow the instructions on pages 6 and 7 to make his headdress but replace the fabric band with a crown cut from holographic card stock.

How to make the king's bag

1 Cut out a rectangle of velvet and fold in half. Sew together the bottom and open side edges with running stitches, leaving open the top end.

2 Use a darning needle to thread a shoe lace or gold embroidery thread near the top of the bag and gather it closed. Loop it over King Herod's arm.

You will need:

Strong, thick card stock

Scissors

Glue and brush

Brown wool

Strong thread

Yellow, white, and brown felt

Large button for eye

Curtain ring

Wooden spoon

How to make a camel

1 Cut out the shape of the camel's head from thick card stock. Cover with a smooth layer of glue. Place the card stock, glue-side down, on top of the felt and firmly rub down on the card stock, especially around the edges.

2 Leave to dry. Trim off the excess felt.

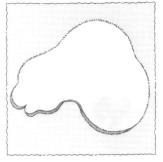

3 Cut lengths of brown wool and glue them in layers to the top of the head to make the camel's mane.

4 Cut out the ear shapes, nostril, and other features from card stock or felt, and glue in place. Use the button to make the eye.

5 Cut two lengths of felt. Glue them to the ring to make the bridle and leave to dry. Position them across the camel's nose and glue the ends to the back.

6 Glue the wooden spoon to the back of the head to act as a handle.

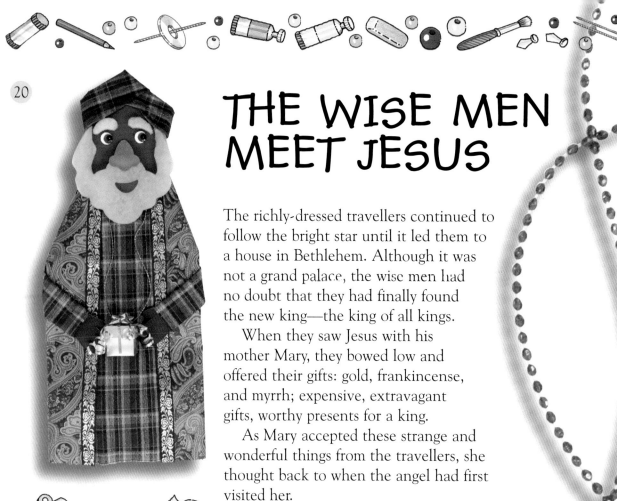

THE WISE MEN MEET JESUS

The richly-dressed travellers continued to follow the bright star until it led them to a house in Bethlehem. Although it was not a grand palace, the wise men had no doubt that they had finally found the new king—the king of all kings.

When they saw Jesus with his mother Mary, they bowed low and offered their gifts: gold, frankincense, and myrrh; expensive, extravagant gifts, worthy presents for a king.

As Mary accepted these strange and wonderful things from the travellers, she thought back to when the angel had first visited her.

"He will be great," the angel had said. "He will reign for ever and his kingdom shall have no end."

"Such a small boy," she wondered, "with so much expected of him from so many different people," and she watched as the wise men left and started on their return journey to their homeland.

You will need:

Small boxes and containers

Empty spice jar

Sheet of gold foil

Ribbons, braid, beads, and bows

Tissue paper

Colored velvet or organza fabric

Rice or potpourri

Colored thread

Colored cord

Scissors, pencil, glue, and brush

Sticky tape

Darning needle

How to make the three gifts

Gold

1 Wrap up a small box or container in gold foil and decorate with bows and ribbons. Tie a length of ribbon to the gift or a string of beads to the box and secure it with sticky tape. Drape it around the neck of one of the wise men.

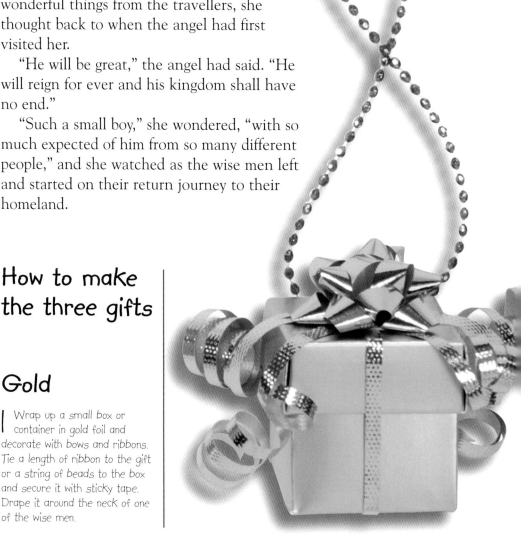

Frankincense

Use the instructions on page 19 to make a bag out of rich colored velvet or organza fabric. Fill it with rice or potpourri and secure the opening with embroidery thread or ribbon. Drape it around the neck of one of the wise men and glue in place in the hands.

Myrrh

Brush an empty spice jar with glue and cover with tissue paper. Smooth down firmly and allow to dry. Decorate with strings of beads and braid and ribbon. Tie on some colored cord or thread and drape it around a wise man's neck.

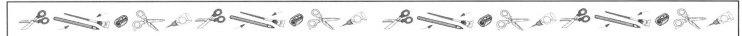

CHRISTMAS PUPPET PLAY SCRIPTS

The angel meets Mary

Enter Mary

Mary: Another hot day in Nazareth. Another hot day of housework. No matter how much I dust and sweep, everywhere just gets dirty again. I can't wait for the vacuum cleaner to be invented. (*Walks back and forth across the stage*) Nothing exciting ever seems to happen here. I wish it would, just once in a while. It's the same thing every day.

Enter angel

Angel: Greetings, Mary! Do not be afraid. My name is Gabriel and I'm an angel.

Mary: (*Looks out to audience*) My mother always said to be careful what you wish for! (*Looks to angel*)

Sorry if I looked a bit shocked, Gabriel. Still, it's understandable. You may well say, "Do not be afraid," but we don't get powerful angels coming to Nazareth every day. Have I done something wrong?

Angel: No Mary, God is pleased with you. You will become pregnant, give birth to a son, and you will call him Jesus. He will be great, and his kingdom will never end.

Mary: But I am not married—although I am engaged to Joseph, the carpenter. How can I have a baby?

Angel: Nothing is impossible with God. Your cousin Elizabeth is expecting her first baby in a few weeks, even though she is very old. This shows God's power. You will be the mother of the Holy One, who will be called the Son of God.

Mary: I can't think why God has chosen me for this. I'm nothing special—just a poor, humble girl. But I am God's servant and I am happy to be part of his plans.

Angel: Peace be with you, Mary! (*Exit*)

Mary: Well, how exciting! And how scary! Still, I do believe that God has marvelous and amazing plans for the world. I wonder if they include getting me some help around the house! I'd better go and find Joseph and tell him the news. (*Exit*)

CHRISTMAS PUPPET PLAY SCRIPT

The census

Enter Mary and Joseph

Mary: Oh, Joseph, I'm so glad that we got married after the angel's news, but now I'm so tired. It's only a few weeks until the baby is due. Do we really have to go all the way to Bethlehem?

Joseph: I'm sorry, Mary, but it's that Caesar Augustus. He's a real control freak. Everyone has to go back to their home town to register.

Mary: But why?

Joseph: So he can sort out the tax collection, I think. Come on, we really ought to get going. It's a long way to walk. Our donkey isn't going to like it.

Mary: Couldn't we have gone by camel train? It's much more comfortable and that donkey of ours is very old and bony.

Joseph: Sorry, everyone is on the move and the train was fully booked. Anyway, it would be much more expensive and we need every shekel for when the baby is born.

Mary: You're right. Look, I've packed a few things and put in some dates and figs for the journey.

Joseph: Great— that'll keep us going. The sooner we start, the sooner we'll get there.

Mary: Yes—and then we can just fall into a nice comfy bed in Bethlehem. It won't be so bad, will it? *(Both exit)*

CHRISTMAS PUPPET PLAY SCRIPT

No room at the inn

The donkey "speaks" to the audience, as if giving a running commentary.

Enter Mary, Joseph, and the donkey

Mary: Oh, Joseph. I don't think I can walk one more step! I'm absolutely worn out.

Donkey *(to audience):* She's worn out! I'm the one who should be complaining; I've carried her most of the way— and just between you and me, she's put on a bit of weight lately.

Joseph: I'm sorry, Mary. We arrived here in Bethlehem in good time, but I didn't realize it was going to be so difficult to find somewhere to stay. Everywhere is completely booked up.

Donkey: I knew they should have packed a tent!

Mary: What shall we do? I'm getting terrible pains in my tummy. I really think I need somewhere to lie down.

Donkey: I thought that fruit looked a bit suspect. Poor thing—I hope she hasn't got a tummy bug.

Joseph: I think I'll go back to that man who owned the inn on the edge of town. He had a very kind face. If I explain everything to him, he may be able to find us somewhere to sleep, even if it's up in the attic. *(Exit Joseph)*

Donkey: I'm not sure that I can manage stairs...

Mary: Oh donkey, what is to become of us? How will we cope with a baby here, with nowhere to stay?

Donkey *(shocked and surprised, still looking to the audience):* A baby? That explains a few things! But what does she mean by "we"? I'm fairly sure I had nothing to do with this!

(Enter Joseph)

Joseph: Good news! That innkeeper has got somewhere for us. The rooms in the inn are all taken but he's going to let us stay somewhere out back. It may be rather simple, but it will have to do.

Mary: Thank goodness. I don't mind where it is. I'm too tired to notice whether it's five-star or not. *(All start to exit)*

Donkey: Five stars? What is she talking about now? There are hundreds of stars in the sky, not just five. And look at that—one enormous one, which seems to be coming our way.

Joseph: Come on donkey—keep up.

Mary: I don't know why we keep talking to that donkey, Joseph. It's not as if he can understand a word we're saying. *(All exit)*

Baby Jesus is born

Enter two cows and the donkey

Donkey (*as if finishing off a conversation*): ... so that was when I led them both to this place. I could see that Mary couldn't walk much further and Joseph was getting worried. Thanks for letting us share the facilities.

Cow 1: It's our pleasure, although it is a bit cramped with all of us in here. I'm only sorry we didn't know in advance. I would have tried to tidy up a bit.

Cow 2: Yes, it's in need of a good cleaning and some new straw.

Donkey: Well, beggars can't be choosers. We've only been here a couple of hours and I'm almost getting used to the smell.

Cow 1 (*moving in front of cow 2*): What are Mary and Joseph doing? It's too dark to see clearly, even though there are lots of stars in the sky. My eyesight isn't what it was.

Cow 2: I can't see because you're right in my way...

Cow 1: Oooh—sorry dear. (*Moves away*)

Cow 2: Mary seems to be holding a baby—but it's ever so small. My Gertrude was a lot bigger than that.

Donkey: That's because you're a cow and you had a calf. This is a baby boy. And isn't he gorgeous?

Cow 1: And look, she's wrapping him up and putting him in our manger. (*sighs in a maternal way*) Aaah.

Cow 2 (*shocked*): In our manger! We've got to have our breakfast out of there tomorrow.

Donkey: Never mind that, just look at the little guy—and look at Mary and Joseph. They obviously adore him.

Cow 1: I wonder what they're going to call him?

Donkey: I think they were talking about Jesus as a possible name.

Cow 2 (*thinking*): Jesus—that means 'the Lord saves' doesn't it?

Cow 1: If you say so. Your education was much better than mine, dear.

Donkey: Well, there's certainly a lot in this world that needs saving. Still, he's got a bit of growing up to do first. He'll have lots of time to do that saving when he's a bit bigger.

Cow 2: Absolutely right. There's one thing for certain—the troubles of this world aren't going anywhere too quickly. (*All exit*)

CHRISTMAS PUPPET PLAY SCRIPT

Angels everywhere!

Enter three shepherds, with sheep bobbing up and down in the background.

Shepherd 1: Do you know what I really hate about being a shepherd?

Shepherd 2 *(thinking)*: Is it that we are stuck up this hill all by ourselves with no one else to talk to?

Shepherd 1: Nope—anyway, there's you two, although sometimes I do get a more interesting conversation from the animals!

Shepherd 3: Is it that there are no showers or baths up here and that everyone smells like their sheep?

Shepherd 1: Nope—but that's on my list!

Shepherd 2: Is it that we are away from home and can't see our children and help them with their homework?

Shepherd 1: Be sensible—I was asking what I hated most about being up here!

Shepherd 3: OK then, we give up—what do you hate most about being a shepherd?

Shepherd 1: Nothing ever happens!

Enter a group of angels from every direction; sheep exit.

Angel group *(randomly)*: Hallelujah; hurrah; glory to God; whoopee!

Shepherds all exit down so only eyes are showing.

Shepherds 2 and 3 *(turning to Shepherd 1)*: You and your big mouth!

Angel 1: Don't be afraid. I bring you good news. Today, down there in Bethlehem, a Savior has been born who is Christ the Lord. You will find him wrapped in cloths and lying in a manger.

Angel group *(as they exit)*: Hallelujah; hurrah; glory to God; whoopee!

Shepherd 1: Have they all gone yet?

Shepherd 2: I think so. What do you make of all that?

Shepherd 3: Well, I was terrified—but I felt as though I was going to burst with joy at the same time.

Shepherds 1 and 2: Me too.

Shepherd 3: So what are we waiting for then? Let's go and find this baby. And one more thing...

Shepherds 1 and 2: What?

Shepherd 3: I don't want to hear anyone saying that nothing ever happens around here! *(All exit)*

CHRISTMAS PUPPET PLAY SCRIPT

The baby in the manger

Enter two shepherds

Shepherd 1: Shame only two of us could come and look for the Savior.

Shepherd 2: Yes—but someone has to stay and look after the sheep.

Shepherd 1: I still can't quite believe what has happened—and why us? Why did those angels come to tell us?

Shepherd 2: I don't know—but what I do know is that I really want to find the baby.

Shepherd 1: Me too—but how? Bethlehem is absolutely packed. And we don't know his name or anything about him!

Shepherd 2: We know that he has been sent by God, so we must trust God to help us find him... Listen.

Shepherd 1: I have been listening. What you say makes a lot of sense for a change and...

Shepherd 2 (*interrupting*): No, no! Don't listen to me—listen to that...

Both shepherds pause, as if listening, and the sound of a baby crying starts.

Shepherds 1 and 2: That's him! (*Both exit*)

Enter Mary and Joseph and manger props

Mary: There, there, little one! I think he's settled now, Joseph.

Joseph: He's got a good pair of lungs on him, that's for sure.

Enter shepherds

Shepherd 1: A good thing he has—otherwise I'm not sure we would have found him!

Shepherd 2 (*looking toward the manger, in wonder*): Our Savior—this tiny baby is our Savior. Praise the Lord!

Joseph: Praise God indeed.

Shepherd 1: He's so small... what have you called him?

Mary: Jesus—we have called him Jesus.

Joseph: How did you know about this?

Shepherd 2: Well, you'll never believe it, but we were visited by angels—masses of them, all singing and telling us that Christ the Lord, our Savior, had been born.

Shepherd 1: It was quite terrifying and we still can't quite believe it ourselves.

Mary: Angels can be quite frightening, can't they—but I'm not sure how else God could send his messages and make sure people believe them.

Shepherd 2: I see what you mean. A letter wouldn't have quite the same impact, would it?

Shepherd 1: And the mail is so unreliable—it may never get there!

Shepherd 2: But we're here and I think that this is the most amazing thing that has ever happened in the world.

Shepherd 1: Absolutely! We must tell everyone else we meet about this.

Shepherd 2: Yes—we may not be angels but we have our voices. Let's go—let's go and tell everyone the most amazing news. Our Savior has been born—Jesus, who is Christ the Lord. (*Shepherds exit*)

CHRISTMAS PUPPET PLAY SCRIPT

Following the star

Enter the wise men and a camel. The camel moves around in the background during the scene.

Wise man 1: Where now?

Wise man 2: Hold on, I'm just checking... *(looks up)*

Wise man 3: You're going to get a terrible pain in the neck doing that.

Wise man 2: Some would say I have two pains in the neck already...

Wise man 1: I still think that having a GPS on one of the camels would have been more reliable than following a star.

Wise man 2: Come on, we all agreed—the sudden appearance of this star is all we need. We have checked the charts and writings, we have plotted a route, and now we are on the way to find him.

Wise man 3: Yes—and I can't wait. I never dreamed that I could be one of the people who was going to meet the King of the world!

Wise man 1: If we ever find him! Look, we have been in Jerusalem for a while now and there is no sign of him here. I say we ask someone.

Wise man 2 *(quickly):* Oh no, I don't think that's necessary.

Wise man 3: No, no, no—after all, we are very important people. We wouldn't want anyone to think that we are... we are...

Wise man 1: Lost?

Wise man 3: Not lost exactly, just temporarily misplaced.

Wise man 1: OK, whatever—but I think I have the answer. Why don't we ask someone as important as us where the new king is?

Wise man 2: Great idea! Jerusalem has a King—what's his name? Harold?

Wise man 3: No, no—and we'd better get his name right. I've heard he has a very short temper and can be very unpredictable. I'm sure he's called Herod. He has quite a reputation.

Wise man 1: And not all of it good!

Wise man 3: Not any of it good!

Wise man 2: Herod, Herod... I think I can remember that.

Wise man 1: I'm sure if he's a great and mighty King he will wish to entertain us at his court.

Wise man 2: Yes, I'm sure he will be able to help us. *(All exit)*

CHRISTMAS PUPPET PLAY SCRIPT

An evil king

Enter King Herod

King Herod (*moving across the stage as he talks to himself*): So, the priests and scribes say that this new King of the Jews, this Messiah, will be born in Bethlehem. (*getting angry*) New King... new King. What am I then? Last year's model? Outdated? Ready for the scrap heap? Out of touch? I'll show them—I'll show them all! (*Calling to off-stage*) Show the wise men in.

Enter wise men.

Wise man 1: Honor to you, King Herod.

Wise man 2: Yes, yes—lots of honor and all that. And I don't believe any of the things people say about you.

Wise man 3 (*hurriedly*): Well, well—thank you so much for seeing us, King Herod. We have heard that you are an all-powerful ruler, so we are sure you will know where the Messiah is.

Herod: I have my sources, and they tell me that he is to be found in Bethlehem. (*innocently*) How exactly did you hear about him, anyway?

Wise man 1: We didn't hear exactly... more see. There's a new star in the sky that is large and bright and seems to be leading us

to him. Bethlehem you say? Well, we'll try there.

Herod: Yes—and I suppose you had better be off? I wouldn't want to delay you any further, when you're on such an important mission.

Wise man 3: Thank you so much, King Herod. You've been a great help.

Wise man 2: Yes—and you're not at all what we expected.

Wise man 1: I think we'd better go quickly.

Wise man 3: Yes—before his big mouth gets us into trouble. (*All start to exit*)

Herod: Have a safe journey... oh and one more thing.

(*Wise men all turn back and say in unison*): Yes?

Herod: If you do find him, could you let me know and tell me where he is?

Wise man 1: Of course, of course. No problem at all.

Herod: After all, I need to find him —a fellow King and all that. (*Wise men have all exited as he speaks*)

Herod: Yes, find him—and kill him! (*Exits*)

CHRISTMAS PUPPET PLAY SCRIPT

Wise men worship

Mary and Joseph, to one side of the set.

Mary: He's such a good boy, isn't he, Joseph?

Joseph: He is, Mary. He's a dear little guy.

Enter the wise men from the other side.

Wise man 1: We have come to worship the Messiah.

Wise man 2: All hail the new King of the Jews.

Wise man 3: We come with gifts for the most worthy child.

Wise man 1: Gold for a King. (*Use gold prop*)

Wise man 2: Frankincense for a priest. (*Use frankincense prop*)

Wise man 3: Myrrh for burial. (*Use myrrh prop*)

Joseph: Thank you for your lavish and unusual gifts. I am sorry that we cannot entertain you in your accustomed style. We are a poor and humble family.

Wise man 1: No matter—we have achieved our aim. We have seen the Messiah and we have paid him homage. We will now leave you in peace. Praise the Lord. (*All exit*)

Mary: Well, what do you make of that, Joseph?

Joseph: Search me. So many strange things have happened lately; I can't keep up with it all, let alone understand it.

Mary: And what odd gifts. Gold, frankincense, and myrrh—most people bring flowers, chocolates, and baby clothes.

Joseph: Yes—but remember what the angel said. This is no ordinary child—he is very special, so I suppose it's only natural that special things will happen.

Mary: You're right and I'm sure that God will be with us to help us know what to do as he grows older.

Joseph: Well, he hasn't let us down yet, has he?

Mary (*laughing*): No, Joseph, he hasn't. Now, maybe we can settle down for a while and concentrate on raising Jesus the way God wants us to (*sound of crying off set*)—oops, there he is again. Now, is it your turn or mine? (*Both exit*)

CHRISTMAS PUPPET PLAY SCRIPT

The dream

Enter the wise men

Wise man 1: Wow! That was amazing! I still can't believe that the new King was in such a humble house with such ordinary people.

Wise man 2: I know what you mean—but it was definitely him. That star was right over the place and when I saw him I just knew this was the right child.

Wise man 3: Me too. Mary and Joseph seemed really overwhelmed by it all, didn't they?

Wise man 1: Not that surprising— I mean, it's not every day that strange foreigners you have never met before, dressed up like Kings, come on a long journey bringing strange birthday presents to your son.

Wise man 3: Well, when you put it like that, I can see what you mean.

Wise man 2: And a new King in such a small house! That other King —Herod—he'll be surprised when we tell him, won't he?

Wise man 1: To be sure—maybe he will invite them to go and live with him at his palace?

Wise man 2: I don't think so —he didn't seem the friendly type.

Wise man 3: Well, we'll find out tomorrow. We can call on him on the way back. Now, I don't know about you, but I'm really tired. Time for sleep.

Wise men 1 and 2: Me too.

All wise men lie down to sleep and start to snore loudly.

Voice-over: You have travelled far and have done well to find the Savior. But King Herod is a ruthless man. He will not allow the new King to live. Do not help Herod. Do not visit him. Find another route home and you will be watched over and kept safe.

Wise men all start to wake up.

Wise man 1: What a terrible night's sleep—I had the most awful dream.

Wise man 2: Not that one you had when you went to bed hungry...

Wise man 3 *(continuing the story)*: Yes, and you dreamed you were eating your turban—the one with the feather in it—and you woke up to find you were chewing your pillow!

Wise man 1: No, it was worse than that.

Wise man 2: Well, it couldn't be as bad as mine.

Wise man 3: Or mine.

Wise man 1: Well, I dreamed that King Herod was going to do the most unspeakable things to the new King.

Wise man 2: Me too—and that he would stop at nothing.

Wise man 3: Mine was the same —it was so frightening to think that one man could destroy the hope we have for the future. We have to find a way to avoid him.

Wise man 1: Well, we have the maps and the camels and all the time in the world to take a longer route home.

Wise man 2: With your map-reading skills, it could be a lot longer than you think. I mean, we haven't got a star to show us the way back.

Wise man 3: Well, let's get going. The sooner we start, the sooner you can get us lost... I mean home.

Wise man 1: Yes, let's load up the camels *(enter camels)* and get going. I don't want to be around when King Herod finds out we've accidentally on purpose forgotten to tell him where Jesus is!

Wise man 2: If he's half as awful as he was in that dream, I want to put as many miles as possible between us and Jerusalem.

Wise man 3: What are we waiting for then—let's go! *(All exit)*

This edition published by Standard Publishing, Cincinnati, Ohio
www.standardpub.com

First edition 2009

Copyright © 2009 Anno Domini Publishing
1 Churchgates, The Wilderness, Berkhamsted, Herts HP4 2UB
www. ad-publishing.com
Story text and plays copyright © 2008 Jane Martin-Scott
Puppet instructions copyright © 2008 Gillian Chapman
Illustrations copyright © 2008 Gillian Chapman

Publishing Director Annette Reynolds
Editor Nicola Bull
Art Director Gerald Rogers
Pre-production Krystyna Kowalska Hewitt
Production John Laister

Printed and bound in Singapore

ISBN 978-0-7847-2335-7